How We Use

Metal

Chris Oxlade

Raintree

Chicago, Illinois

For information, address the publisher:
Raintree
100 N. LaSalle, Suite 1200
Chicago, IL 60602

Originated by Ambassador Litho
Printed and bound in China by
South China Printing Company

09 08 07 06 05
10 9 8 7 6 5 4 3 2 1

Library of Congress Cataloging-in-Publication Data
Oxlade, Chris.
 How we use metal / Chris Oxlade.
   p. cm. -- (Using materials)
 Includes bibliographical references and index.
 ISBN 1-4109-0602-7 -- ISBN 1-4109-0893-3
 1. Metals--Juvenile literature. I. Title. II. Series.
 TA459.O85 2004
 620.1'6--dc22

                              2004002915

Acknowledgments
The publisher would like to thank the following
for permission to reproduce photographs: p. 4
(H. Rogers) Trip; pp. 5 (Maximilian Stock Ltd), 6
(Publiphoto Diffusion/P. G. Adam), 10 (Pascal
Goetgheluk), 11 (Tek Image), 12 (Alex Bartel), 13
(Tony Craddock), 15 (Tek Image), 16 (Andrew
Syred), 21 (Adrienne Hart-Davis), 28 (John Mead),
29 (John Mead) Science Photo Library; pp. 8
(Trip/David Tarrant), 9 (Trip/Martin Barlow), 25
(Trip/John Wender) Art Directors; pp. 7 (Harcourt
Index), 14 (Owaki-Kulla), 19 (Harcourt
Education), 22 (Harcourt Education), 24 (George
Diebold), 27 (Owen Franken) Corbis; p. 17 Trevor
Clifford; p. 18 Ecoscene; p. 20 Alamy; p. 23
photolibrary.com; p. 26 Tudor Photography.

Cover photograph of metal ventilation pipes
reproduced with permission of Getty Images.

Every effort has been made to contact copyright
holders of any material reproduced in this book.
Any omissions will be rectified in subsequent
printings if notice is given to the publishers.

Contents

Some words are shown in bold, **like this.** You can find out what they mean by looking in the glossary.

Metals and Their Properties

All the things we use are made from **materials.** Metals are materials. There are many different types of metals. We use metals for thousands of different jobs. Metals are used to make engines and huge buildings. Metal nuts and bolts join things together. Some metals are used to make beautiful jewelry.

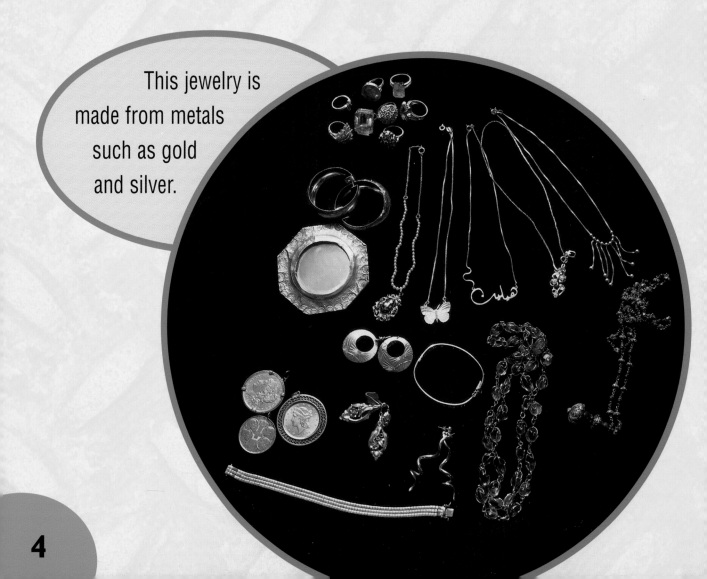

This jewelry is made from metals such as gold and silver.

Huge pieces of metal are used to build a ship.

The **properties** of a material tell us what it is like. One property of many metals is that they are hard and strong. Most metals must be heated to a very high **temperature** before they melt. All metals are shiny. They all **conduct** electricity and heat. Some metals can be made into **magnets.**

Do not use it!

The properties of materials make them useful for some jobs. The properties also make them not good for other jobs. For example, sheets of metal do not bend easily. This is one reason we do not use metal to make clothes.

Where Do Metals Come From?

Most metals come from **natural raw materials.** These raw materials are rocks from Earth's **crust.** The rocks that contain metals are called **ores.** For example, we get aluminum from an ore called bauxite. Ores are dug from mines. Most ore mines are giant holes in the ground.

Copper ore is dug from the ground at this mine in Arizona.

This molten iron has been made by smelting iron ore.

Metals are locked tightly in ores. We cannot get them out by smashing up the ores. We have to use **chemicals** and a lot of heat instead. This is called **smelting.** For example, to get iron from iron ore we heat the ore to more than 1830° Fahrenheit (1000° Celsius). **Coke** and **limestone** are added to remove the other chemicals from the ore, leaving **molten** iron.

Metals in the past

In the past, people used only metals that were easy to get from rocks. People have made things from gold for about 10,000 years. This is because pure gold was found in lumps. People began to use copper and tin about 6,000 years ago and iron about 3,000 years ago.

Metals in Machines

Most metals are tough. They do not break when we flatten, stretch, or bend them. They are good for making things that have to be very strong. Think about a bicycle. Its frame is made from aluminum tubes, and its wheels are made from **steel.**

Many metals are also very hard. It is difficult to mark the surface of these metals. Things made from these metals last a long time. We use hard metals to make things that will be rubbed, scraped, or hit.

Machine parts such as these ball bearings are made from steel.

Scientists say that metals are
elastic. This means metals can
stretch and bend slightly and then
go back into shape. We cannot normally see these
movements because they are very small. We can see
them in springs, which can be squeezed and stretched
a lot. We use springs in many machines and objects. Tiny
springs are found in watches. Huge springs are used in
trucks and trains. Springs can be stretched and
squashed thousands of times without breaking.

The metal springs on this
train take up bumps
from the tracks.

Metals in the Home

The strength and hardness of metals makes them good **materials** for making tools such as hammers, wrenches, and screwdrivers. Kitchen knives are made from metal so that they do not break when you cut food. We also use metals for nuts, bolts, nails, screws, hinges, and brackets.

Saw blades are also made from metal.

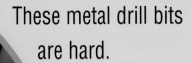

These metal drill bits are hard.

For some jobs we need metals to be very hard. One way to make a metal harder is to add other metals to it. This makes it an **alloy.** Tools such as wrenches are made from an alloy that contains the metals **steel,** chromium, and vanadium. This alloy is almost impossible to scratch or dent. We also make metals harder by heating them until they are red hot. Then we dip them in cold water to cool them quickly. This is called tempering.

Do not use it!

A piece of metal is heavier than a similar-sized piece of most other materials, such as plastic. This means that objects made of certain metals are very heavy. So we do not use these metals to make things that must be lightweight, such as suitcases.

Metals for Building

Many buildings have **steel** frames that hold up their walls and roofs. The frame is made of **columns** and **beams.** They are joined together with steel nuts and bolts. The frame is made from a very strong type of steel. Many bridges are also made using steel beams. A suspension bridge is held up by thick, strong steel cables.

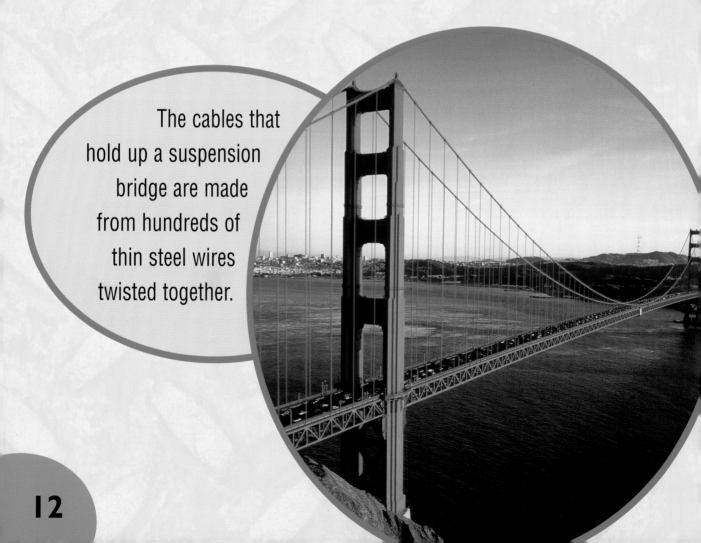

The cables that hold up a suspension bridge are made from hundreds of thin steel wires twisted together.

Steel frames are used when putting up tall buildings.

In buildings we also use steel with **concrete.** The concrete sets around a frame of steel bars. The steel and concrete together are called reinforced concrete. It is a very strong **material.** The tallest buildings in the world are built using reinforced concrete.

Do not use it!

Not all metals are useful for building. Some metals, such as copper, are soft and bendable. We do not use them for making building frames because they are not strong enough.

Shaping Metals

We can change the shape of a piece of metal by hammering it. For example, if you step on an empty aluminum drink can, you can crush it. We could not do this with a **material** such as glass. Glass would shatter into pieces. A piece of metal can also be stretched to make it long and thin. For example, we can make a thin metal wire by carefully pulling a metal rod.

A blacksmith uses a hammer to shape hot metal.

Metals can be made into shapes when they are hot or cold. Casting is making a metal object by pouring **molten** metal into a mold. Hammering and rolling metals into shape is easier when the metals are heated until they are red hot and soft. When metals are cold, they can be cut with saws and drills. Sheets of metal can also be pressed into shapes such as baking trays and car body panels.

These workers are pouring molten metal into a mold.

Metals for Electricity

All metals allow electricity to flow through them. We say that they **conduct** electricity. Copper is used to make wires that carry electricity from one place to another. Copper is a soft metal. For this reason, copper wires are easy to bend around corners. We also use copper to make **circuit boards** for computers and calculators. Power cables that carry electricity to our homes have a metal called aluminum in them. This is because aluminum is light, bendable, and easy to put in cables.

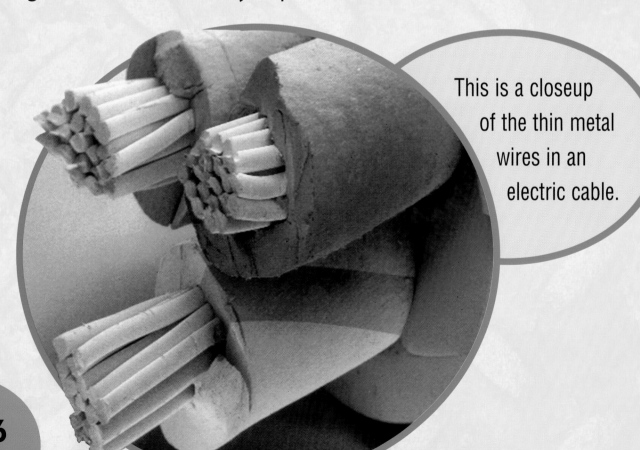

This is a closeup of the thin metal wires in an electric cable.

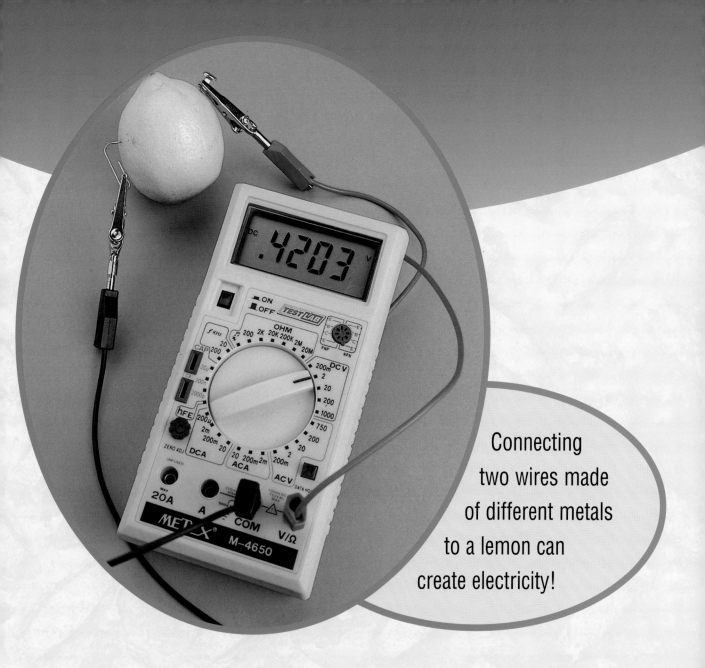

Connecting
two wires made
of different metals
to a lemon can
create electricity!

We also use metals to make electricity. Batteries always contain metals. Inside a battery, two different metals work together to make electricity. For example, a ni-cad battery contains the metals nickel and cadmium. Ni-cad batteries are **rechargeable** and are used in cell phones and battery-powered toys.

Metals for Magnets

The metals iron, cobalt, and nickel are very special. They are the only metals that can be made magnetic. Things made from these metals are attracted to **magnets.** We can also make magnets from these metals.

For example, we can make an iron bar into a magnet by stroking it with another magnet.

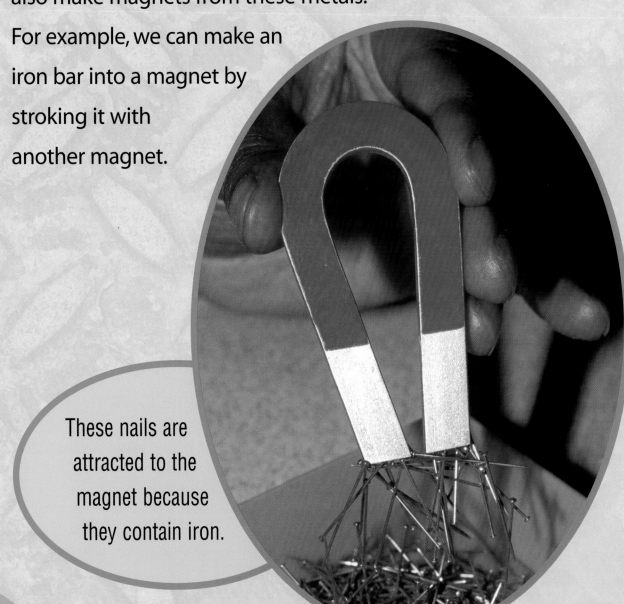

These nails are attracted to the magnet because they contain iron.

A compass needle is made of iron or **steel.**

Magnets and **electromagnets** have dozens of uses. Refrigerator magnets are very simple. We use them to hold pieces of paper on the door of a refrigerator. The needle in a compass is a magnet. It always swings around to point north because Earth works like a giant magnet. Electric motors, **dynamos,** and loudspeakers contain magnets, too.

Metals and Heat

Most metals melt only at high **temperatures.** That means we have to make them very hot before they turn from a **solid** to a **liquid.** This is why we use metals to make objects that get hot, such as ovens and barbecues. We also use metals to make parts of machines that get hot, such as car exhausts. Other **materials,** such as plastic, would melt if they were used.

A jet engine can reach a temperature of 5,100° F (2,800° C)!

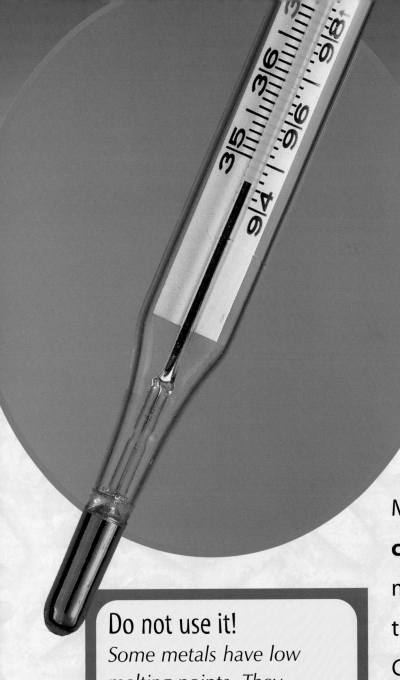

This thermometer uses mercury, but digital thermometers are safer.

Metals are also good at **conducting** heat. This means that heat flows through metals well. Cooking pans are made from metals such as **steel,** aluminum, and copper. Heat from the stove moves through the metal to the food in the pan.

Do not use it!

Some metals have low melting points. They would melt in an oven, so we do not use them to make pots and pans. Mercury is a unusual metal because it is a liquid at room temperature. We have to cool it down to make it into a solid.

Mixing Metals

We often use metals on their own for jobs. For example, we make some cooking pans from copper. Copper dents and bends easily. We can improve the **properties** of metals by mixing them with other metals or **materials.** These new metals are called **alloys.** For example, nickel is added to copper to make copper harder. We use this alloy to make coins.

This doorknob is made from brass, an alloy of copper and zinc.

Strong steel cables are used in cranes, elevators, and many other machines.

Steel is the metal we use most. Steel is not a pure metal. It is an alloy. It is made by mixing a tiny amount of carbon, which is not a metal, with **molten** iron. A thin rod of pure iron is soft and easy to bend. Steel is much harder and stronger than pure iron. We use steel in buildings, ships, car bodies, and machine parts.

Do not use it!

Some alloys contain metals that are hard to find. This means that they cost a lot to make. We do not use these alloys or rare metals such as platinum to make everyday objects. Instead, we use cheap metals such as iron and steel for these jobs.

Metals, Water, and Air

If an object made from iron or **steel** gets damp, it will quickly turn brown. The brown substance is called rust. If the metal stays damp, it will gradually be eaten away by rust. Then it will turn weak and crumbly. Rusting is an example of a process called corrosion. Other metals **corrode** when they get damp, too. Some metals, such as gold and titanium, do not corrode at all.

Eventually, rust will make this iron chain crumble to dust.

Steel cans are coated with tin to stop them from rusting.

Rust makes things weak, so it is important to stop things from rusting. One way to prevent rusting is to stop water from reaching a metal. We can do this by covering the surface of the metal with oil or paint. We can also cover it with a layer of a metal that does not rust, such as zinc or chrome. A special type of steel called stainless steel does not rust. It is an **alloy** of steel, nickel, and chromium. We use it to make sinks, cutlery, and countertops.

Do not use it!

For some jobs we cannot use metals that corrode. For example, a replacement hip joint made of metal must not corrode inside a person's body. Instead, we use metals that do not corrode, such as titanium.

Metals for Decoration

All metals are shiny when they are freshly cut and polished. They also come in different colors. For example, aluminum is shiny and gray. Brass is shiny and yellow. We use the shine and color of metals for decoration. For example, we make ornaments from brass and light fittings from aluminum.

This light fitting is made from polished metal.

These medals were awarded for bravery in wartime.

Jewelry can be made from gold or silver. These metals have beautiful colors and are very shiny. They are also soft metals that are easy to cut and shape into jewelry. Some jewelry is made of a cheaper metal, such as brass, with a thin coat of gold or silver on top. This is called gold plate or silver plate.

Do not use it!

*We do not use metals that **corrode**, such as iron, to make jewelry. It rusts easily and does not look shiny. However, some sculptures are made from copper because copper turns green as it corrodes.*

Metals and the Environment

Throwing metals away can cause problems for the environment. Metals do not rot away quickly like some other **materials,** such as wood. Rusting cars, food cans, and other metals fill up garbage dumps. There, they can harm animals and people. Some metals are poisonous. Mercury is the only metal that is a **liquid** at room **temperature.** We use it for many jobs. However, it can poison fish and people if it gets into rivers.

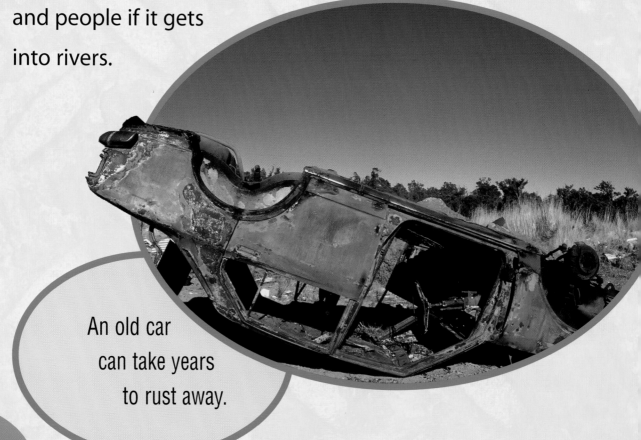

An old car can take years to rust away.

These aluminum cans will be recycled.

Metals such as **steel,** aluminum, and gold can be **recycled.** We can melt objects made from these metals and make them into new objects. Recycling metals is good for the environment. Mining and **smelting** metals uses huge amounts of **energy,** which comes from burning fuels. If we recycle metals, we save this energy and the pollution it causes. Digging to find more **ores** can be avoided by recycling. This can save habitats where plants and animals live, too.

Find Out for Yourself

The best way to find out more about metals is to investigate them for yourself. Look around your home for things made from metal, and keep an eye out for metal during your day. Think about why metal was used to make each object. What properties make it a good material to use? You will find the answers to many of your questions in this book. You can also look in other books and on the Internet.

Books to read

Baldwin, Carol. *Metals*. Chicago: Raintree, 2004.

Ballard, Carol. *Science Answers: Electricity*. Chicago: Heinemann Library, 2004.

Ballard, Carol. *Science Answers: Grouping Materials*. Chicago: Heinemann Library, 2004.

Ballard, Carol. *Science Answers: Magnetism*. Chicago: Heinemann Library, 2004.

Bryant-Mole, Karen, and Mir Tamim Ansary. *Magnets*. Chicago: Heinemann Library, 2002.

Donald, Rhonda Lucas. *Recycling*. Danbury, Conn.: Scholastic Library, 2001.

Hunter, Rebecca. *Discovering Science: Matter*. Chicago: Raintree, 2003.

Parker, Steve. *Electricity and Magnetism*. Langhorne, Pa.: Chelsea House, 2004.

Pluckrose, Henry. *Find Out About Metal*. New York: Franklin Watts, 2002.

Using the Internet

Explore the Internet to find out more about metals. Have an adult help you use a search engine. Type in keywords such as *iron smelting, copper,* or *magnets*.

Glossary

alloy material made from two or more metals or a metal and another material

beam horizontal piece of a frame, supported at each end

chemical substance that we use to make other substances, or for jobs such as cleaning

circuit board set of wires that is designed to carry electricity for a certain purpose

coke fuel made by heating coal

column vertical piece of a frame

concrete material made from cement and gravel

conduct carry or transmit heat or electricity

corrode be slowly eaten away

crust layer of solid rock that forms Earth's outer layer

dynamo device that makes electricity as it spins

elastic able to stretch and return to its original shape

electromagnet iron bar, with wire coiled around it. It becomes a magnet when electricity flows through the wire.

energy power to do work

limestone type of rock that is formed from animal remains and that is used in building

liquid something in a runny state that can be poured from one container to another

magnet material that attracts iron

material matter that things are made from

molten melted

natural anything that is not made by people

ore rock that we get metals from

property characteristic or quality of a material

raw material material that we get other materials from or that we make into other materials

rechargeable battery that we can put electricity back into after using it

recycle use again

smelting process of getting metals from their ores

solid having a fixed shape and size

steel alloy of iron and carbon

temperature measure of how hot or cold something is

Index